THE Little Book of NEWFOUNDLAND & LABRADOR

JOHN SYLVESTER

NIMBUS
PUBLISHING LTD

ACKNOWLEDGMENT:

Special thanks to Gillian Marx of Newfoundland
& Labrador Tourism for her assistance.

Nimbus Publishing Limited
3731 Mackintosh St, Halifax, NS B3K 5A5
(902) 455-4286 nimbus.ca

Printed and bound in China

NB1205

Cover and interior design: Jenn Embree
Front cover ∼ Waves lash the rugged cliffs at Sleepy Cove, near Twillingate.
Back cover ∼ An iceberg drifts beneath dramatic evening clouds near Fogo Island.

Library and Archives Canada Cataloguing in Publication

Sylvester, John, 1955-, photographer
The little book of Newfoundland and Labrador / John Sylvester.
ISBN 978-1-77108-370-6 (bound)
1. Newfoundland and Labrador—Pictorial works. I. Title.

FC2162.S95 2016   971.8022'2   C2015-907612-9

Canada Council   Conseil des arts
for the Arts   du Canada

Nimbus Publishing acknowledges the financial support for its publishing activities from the Government of Canada through the Canada Book Fund (CBF) and the Canada Council for the Arts, and from the Province of Nova Scotia. We are pleased to work in partnership with the Province of Nova Scotia to develop and promote our creative industries for the benefit of all Nova Scotians.

For my good friend Blaine Hrabi who has shared so
many memorable journeys.

Introduction

MY LOVE AFFAIR WITH NEWFOUNDLAND AND LABRADOR BEGAN more than thirty years ago when a friend and I spent a two-week summer sojourn exploring Canada's easternmost province by car. Since then, I've returned again and again; sometimes on assignment, but just as often on personal journeys of exploration to photograph the unique beauty of this remarkable place, and accept the generous hospitality of its people.

Newfoundland and Labrador are just that: two places. There is the island of Newfoundland, affectionately referred to as "The Rock" by residents (where 98 per cent of the province's 527,000 residents live), and Labrador, which is part of Canada's mainland. Together they comprise 405,720 square kilometers of territory, more than three times the size of the other three Atlantic provinces combined. There is much to explore.

It is a place defined by the sea. Where "fish" means cod and, for more than four hundred years, the people relied mainly on "fish" for their livelihood, venturing out in small boats from the hundreds of tiny communities that dotted the province's coastline to harvest the ocean's bounty.

On that first trip in 1982, I pitched my tent on a hillside overlooking a picturesque fishing village on Trinity Bay and awoke to the sound of screen doors slapping. I poked my head out of the tent to the sight of fishers ambling down narrow lanes to their boats. My friend and I scrambled out of our sleeping bags and hurried down to the wharf where we were immediately invited to join two fishers as they checked their elaborate nets, called cod traps. We spent an idyllic morning on the water watching those stalwart men of the sea haul cod from their traps against a backdrop of somber gray cliffs.

That way of life ended in 1992 when the cod moratorium shut down the province's inshore fishery, throwing thousands of people out of work and shrinking

FACING ∾ Fading memories on Change Islands.

coastal towns and villages. Since then, these communities have had to reinvent themselves. Some are finding new life as destinations for travellers drawn to the unspoiled natural beauty and unique cultural experience that only Newfoundland and Labrador can offer.

One of the main attractions for many visitors—and especially for photographers—is the annual parade of icebergs that drift past Newfoundland and Labrador between April and August. Calved from the Greenland ice cap, these 10,000-year-old behemoths drift south along the coast, many running aground along the province's ragged coastline. Their sculpted forms are like exclamation marks punctuating an already rich coastal narrative.

During one especially good iceberg season, I travelled to Twillingate, the self-declared "Iceberg Capital of the World." I asked the proprietor of the bed and breakfast where I was staying if she could recommend someone to take me by boat to photograph them in the evening light. "My daughter's boyfriend has a boat," she offered. A few hours later, the young boatman and I were skimming over the calm waters of Notre Dame Bay in his small outboard-powered punt. It was a lovely evening and I was delighted to photograph several beautifully sculpted icebergs bathed in warm sunset light. Each time we moved the boat, he cut the engine to reduce vibration while I photographed. In order to restart the engine, however, he had to repeatedly pull the starter cord, and eventually pulled the cord right out of the engine! "Not to worry," he said, and started rowing—and telling stories. He spoke proudly of his grandfather who still cut his own firewood by hand, refusing to use a chainsaw because it "wasted wood."

Later that evening, when I finally arrived back at the bed and breakfast, my hosts offered me a nightcap of rum with iceberg ice in it. The ice popped and fizzed in my drink as the 10,000-year-old air bubbles escaped. It was just another day filled with the exceptional experiences that I've come to expect in Newfoundland and Labrador. It's what keeps me coming back, again and again.

FACING ∿ The community of Tilting, on Fogo Island, dates back to the 1730s when the first Irish settlers arrived on its shores. Today, visitors can wander past restored buildings and gardens that offer a rare glimpse of the inshore fishery past of a traditional Newfoundland outport. Tilting was designated a National Historic Site of Canada in 2003.

ABOVE :~ Jim Edwards, a fisher and boat builder, takes a break from building a punt in his shop on Change Islands. There has been a renaissance in punt building on Change and Fogo Islands since the establishment of the annual punt races between the two islands every summer.

BELOW :~ Every spring and summer a parade of icebergs, calved from Greenland's ice cap, drift south along the shores of Newfoundland and Labrador.

ABOVE ∻ Fishers from the village of Durrell motor out into Notre Dame Bay to check their lobster traps

FACING ∻ Winter lingers on Change Islands, where a May snowfall dusts the landscape.

OVERLEAF ∻ Twilight casts its glow over Back Harbour, near Twillingate.

ABOVE :~ A grounded iceberg dwarfs a passing boat in Notre Dame Bay.

FACING ABOVE :~ Situated more than one hundred metres above sea level on a cliff named Devils Cove Head, Long Point Lighthouse has a commanding view over Notre Dame Bay. It's a perfect location for spotting icebergs.

FACING BELOW :~ Evening light graces a tranquil coastal scene near Durrell.

FACING :~ Sunrise palette over Spillars Cove.

BELOW :~ Waves lash the rugged cliffs at Sleepy Cove, near Twillingate.

FACING :~ The root cellars in Elliston harken back to an era before electricity, when these earthen structures were used to store root vegetables, a crucial contribution to the diet of fishing families trying to survive on this rugged coast. Today, more than one hundred root cellars remain in the Elliston area, prompting its declaration as "The Root Cellar Capital of the World."

BELOW AND BELOW FACING :~ Breathtaking coastal views reward hikers who explore the community trails surrounding the picturesque fishing village of Salvage on Bonavista Bay.

FACING AND ABOVE :~ The spire of the historic St. Paul's Anglican Church, built in 1894, dominates the skyline in Trinity. For centuries, the village was an important centre for the thriving fishery, lumbering, and shipbuilding industries. Trinity's remarkably preserved architectural heritage—and popular summer theatre festival—attracts thousands of visitors each year.

ABOVE :~ A shifting fog bank slowly reveals the outline of hills and rocky shore in Trinity Bay.

FACING :~ The Cape Bonavista Lighthouse was constructed in 1843. The historic red-striped structure is a landmark known for its unique architecture, with the lightkeepers' residence built right around the tower. It still houses the original lamp and reflector, which were installed in the early nineteenth century.

ABOVE ∾ "A mausey day," means it's a foggy, wet, and windy one along the rocky coast at Elliston Point.

FACING ∾ Ocean and river meet at the mouth of Anchor Brook near Musgrave Harbour.

ABOVE AND FACING ∻ The Atlantic puffin is the provincial bird of Newfoundland and Labrador. The colourful seabirds are found in many locations throughout the province, and nest primarily on inaccessible offshore islands. At Elliston Point, however, visitors can enjoy excellent cliffside views of the puffins during their May to September nesting season.

OVERLEAF ∻ Sts. Peter and Paul Parish stands prominently overlooking the village of Kings Cove on Bonavista Bay.

ABOVE :~ At day's end, a fishing boat returns to safe harbour in Flowers Cove on the northern peninsula.

FACING :~ In the fishing village of Kings Cove, lobster traps are loaded and ready for setting in the waters of Bonavista Bay.

ABOVE :~ A bull moose browses along the roadside near St. Anthony. There are over 100,000 moose roaming the island of Newfoundland, all descended from four individuals who were imported to the island from New Brunswick in 1904.

RIGHT :~ Woodland caribou once roamed by the thousands throughout Newfoundland and Labrador. Their numbers have diminished in recent years, but watchful travellers driving the Irish Loop through the southern Avalon Peninsula may still spot them grazing the barrens near Trepassey.

FACING :~ The low-lying shrubs *Diapensia lapponica* (commonly known as the pincushion plant) and *Phyllodoce caerulea* (blue mountain heath) are hardy inhabitants of the Labrador tundra. Their tiny delicate flowers emerge in late June.

FACING AND LEFT :~ Cape St. Mary's Ecological Reserve is Newfoundland and Labrador's most accessible seabird colony. During the breeding season (April to October) visitors can witness tens of thousands of birds nesting, perching, diving, soaring, and wheeling through the sky just metres away. There are many seabird species to see here, but majestic northern gannets are the undisputed stars of the show.

BELOW :~ Waves thrash the beach at Sandbanks Provincial Park in the aftermath of an autumn storm on Newfoundland's southwest coast.

FACING ∿ The sun's rays pierce storm clouds over Three Rock Cove on the Port au Port Peninsula.

BELOW ∿ A seemingly endless row of lobster traps stacked on the beach at Three Rock Cove.

ABOVE ∿ The distinctive Rose Blanche Lighthouse commands a magnificent view over the surrounding coastline. Built in 1871 from local granite, the tower was designed by the D&T Stevenson Company, lighthouse engineers from Scotland, which was named after the father and uncle of author Robert Louis Stevenson.

FACING ∿ Barachois Falls tumbles more than fifty metres over the rocky barrens near Rose Blanche on Newfoundland's rugged southwest coast.

BELOW :~ In 1963, in his book *The Road Across Canada,* travel writer Ed McCourt described Rose Blanche as fulfilling "our dreams of what a Newfoundland village ought to look like." Its colourful charms are still on display today for those who take the forty-five-minute drive east from the ferry terminal at Port aux Basques.

FACING ABOVE AND BELOW :~ The last service to be held at Bethany United Church was in September 2003. Built in 1859, the designated heritage structure is said to be one of the province's oldest wooden churches. The outport in which it stands, The Petites, is located on Newfoundland's southwest coast and was resettled in October 2003. Most of its residents moved to nearby Rose Blanche.

OVERLEAF :~ Just minutes away from the ferry terminal at Port aux Basques, Cape Ray is good place to explore the rocky coastline and listen to the roar of the waves.

ABOVE ∻ Spectacular coastal scenery and curious sheep are just two of the sights that greet hikers along the Green Gardens Trail in Gros Morne National Park of Canada.

FACING ∻ The fishing community of Trout River is located at the southern end of Gros Morne National Park of Canada, in the shadow of the Tablelands.

⚜ *JOHN SYLVESTER*

FACING :~ In early July, blue flag iris (*Iris versicolor*) bloom along the Green Garden Trail in Gros Morne National Park of Canada.

BELOW :~ Waves surge around sunset-tinged boulders at Lobster Cove in Gros Morne National Park of Canada.

ABOVE ↜ Scudding cumulus clouds over Trout River Pond and the Tablelands in Gros Morne National Park of Canada.

FACING ↜ The dramatic view of Ten Mile Pond and surrounding Long Range Mountains is a well-deserved reward for those who climb the James Callaghan Trail to the top of Gros Morne Mountain.

OVERLEAF ↜ Shear cliffs of the Tablelands are reflected in a tide pool at Neddy Harbour on Bonne Bay.

ABOVE :∽ The Norris Point lookout offers visitors a glorious view of Bonne Bay and the Tablelands of Gros Morne National Park of Canada.

FACING :∽ One of the most popular excursions in Gros Morne National Park is the boat tour of Western Brook Pond; a glacial carved, 16-kilometre-long freshwater lake. Passengers crane their necks at the soaring cliffs and awe-inspiring waterfalls, including Pissing Mare Falls: at 350 metres, this waterfall is among the highest in eastern North America.

ABOVE ∿ Spring runoff from melting snow tumbles over the barren Tablelands in Gros Morne National Park. The distinctive rock of the area, peridotite, was forced up from the earth's mantle during a plate collision several hundred million years ago. It is devoid of nutrients required for plant growth, thus the lack of vegetation in the area.

FACING ∿ Arches Provincial Park, which is just north of Gros Morne National Park, features a distinctive natural limestone formation created by relentless waves over millions of years.

FACING :~ Flyfishers try their luck casting for Atlantic salmon on the Torrent River. The renowned salmon river is located near Hawkes Bay on the Great Northern Peninsula.

BELOW :~ Visitors to the Salmon Interpretation Centre on the Torrent River can experience a face-to-fin encounter with wild Atlantic salmon in the underwater viewing chamber.

ABOVE :~ Fishing rod and hip waders adorn the cabin rail at Tuckamore Lodge on the Great Northern Peninsula while a "sport" takes a break from casting for salmon in nearby rivers.

FACING :~ Welcoming and guiding lights greet the evening at Quirpon Island Lighthouse Inn.

ABOVE :~ Over one thousand years ago, Vikings from Greenland established an encampment at the northern tip of Newfoundland's Great Northern Peninsula, which they called Vinland. Today, L'Anse aux Meadows is recognized as a UNESCO World Heritage Site and the only authenticated Norse site in North America. A popular attraction at the site is the replica sod-and-timber Viking longhouse.

FACING ABOVE LEFT :~ Doris Roberts greets guests with a smile and freshly baked bread at Quirpon Island Lighthouse Inn.

FACING ABOVE RIGHT :~ Earl Pilgrim, renowned author and conservationist, has written more than a dozen books telling the stories and history of the Great Northern Peninsula, where he has lived for most of his life.

FACING BELOW :~ Conche is an isolated community on the eastern shore of the Great Northern Peninsula with a rich fishing history dating back to the eighteenth century when both French and English fleets used it as a base. The white crosses adorning the doors of many of Conche's buildings are a cultural motif unique to the region, known locally as the "French Shore."

FACING :~ A lone kayaker gets a close-up view of an iceberg in the waters off the Great Northern Peninsula.

BELOW :~ A pair of humpback whales spout in the waters off Quirpon Island. From June to September, the waters surrounding Newfoundland and Labrador host the world's largest gathering of humpbacks which come to feed on a smorgasbord of capelin, krill, and squid.

OVERLEAF :~ Sunlight filters through heavy fog to gild sculpted icebergs off the Great Northern Peninsula.

ABOVE ∾ Icebergs end their journey from Greenland's glaciers in the waters off Newfoundland and Labrador, breaking up and eventually melting into the Atlantic Ocean. Here, grounded bergs and shattered ice clog Greenspond Tickle.

FACING ∾ The colourful tapestry of downtown St. John's, North America's oldest city.

FACING :~ The colourful wooden row houses in St. John's are affectionately known as "Jellybean Row."

BELOW :~ Fog shrouds the Battery, a collection of houses clinging to the cliffs at the entrance to St. John's Harbour. It was once a fishing community within city limits; today the fishing boats are gone, but the town's unique charm endures with its narrow lanes and colourful houses.

ABOVE ∿ Unloading the catch in Petty Harbour.

FACING ∿ Cape Spear is the most easterly point on the North American continent, closer to Ireland than to all of mainland Canada west of Toronto. Two lighthouses stand sentinel on its rugged cliffs with a panoramic views of the surrounding ocean. The cement tower pictured here was built in 1955 to replace the decommissioned historic stone and wood lighthouse.

FACING :~ Battle Harbour, Labrador, was once the thriving centre of the Labrador cod fishery. It is also the place from which Robert Peary sent news to the world that he had reached the North Pole in 1909. Today, this designated National Historic District of Canada offers nostalgic accommodations and dining for travellers who wish to journey back to an earlier time.

BELOW :~ A hiker takes in the view of Saglek Bay in Labrador's Torngat Mountains National Park. The park is included in the Inuit territory known as Nunatsiavut, which appropriately means "Our Beautiful Land."

OVERLEAF :~ Polar bears are frequently sighted along the rocky coast of northern Labrador. They sometimes drift south on the ice pack, and make the news when they wander into coastal communities on the island of Newfoundland.

FACING :~ Weathered and abandoned buildings in Hebron once housed Hudson's Bay Company employees who traded with local Inuit.

BELOW :~ Joseph (Buddy) and Jenny Merkuratsuk greet visitors to Hebron on the Labrador coast. The Inuit couple and their two sons spend summers at their camp in the abandoned community, which was once the northernmost settlement in Labrador and the site of a Moravian Mission from 1831 until 1959, when the community was relocated.

OVERLEAF :~ A timeless outport scene on Change Islands in Notre Dame Bay.

ABOVE :~ Cotton grass thrives in the wetlands of Southwest Arm, Saglek Bay, surrounded by the jagged peaks of Torngat Mountains National Park.